MW01206111

101 Useful Notary Tips

NATIONAL NOTARY ASSOCIATION

Published by:

National Notary Association
9350 De Soto Ave.
Chatsworth, CA 91311-4926
Telephone: (818) 739-4000
Fax: (818) 700-0920
Website: www.NationalNotary.org
Email: nna@NationalNotary.org

Copyright © 2010 National Notary Association
ALL RIGHTS RESERVED. No part of this publication may be reproduced
or used in any form without written permission from the publisher.

Third Edition, Second Printing

ISBN 978-1-59767-082-1
Illustrations by Howard Fullmer and James Veo

TABLE OF CONTENTS

Welcome to 101 Useful Notary Tips.

The many topics covered in this book give you a general overview of the aspects and issues affecting Notaries, providing you with an understanding of the important principles of notarization.

These tips have been taken from our publications, *The National Notary* magazine and *Notary Bulletin* newspaper, now an eNews publication, and describe situations that are common among the 50 states and U.S. possessions.

As a result, the information in this book is general in nature, and may, therefore, conflict with specific state laws. Always check with your state's laws to ensure you comply with the procedures specific to your state.

ACHNOWLEDGMENTS

1 Verbal Requirements

How exactly do you take an acknowledgment?

Are there any special words that have to be recited? Not really, although it would certainly be helpful if a signer walked up to your desk saying something like, "I acknowledge that this is my signature and I affixed it without duress." But how often does that happen?

In most cases, the very act of approaching a Notary, saying, "I'd like to get my signature notarized," and handing over the signed document suffices as an acknowledgment. However, nothing prevents you from asking, "Is this your freely made signature?" ∎

2 Out-Of-State Certificates

May you fill out an acknowledgment certificate from another state if it comes with a given document, or must you always use the forms prescribed by your state's law?

That depends. If the out-of-state certificate is "substantially compliant" with the required or customary acknowledgment form for your state — and most of the time it will be — go ahead and use it. If it's not or you aren't sure, use a form prescribed by your own state.

Before you replace any certificate, however, explain to the signer why you're not using the acknowledgment form that came with the document. That can help avert automatic rejection of your certificate in the other state. ∎

ALTERATIONS & CORRECTIONS

APOSTILLES

3 Initial Changes

Any change written on a legal document should be initialed by all parties signing the document.

Any change written on a notarial certificate should be initialed by the Notary. ■

4 Correct the Certificate Yourself

If someone calls back after a notarization and tells you that you've made a mistake in filling out a notarial certificate, tell them that you, and you alone, must correct that certificate.

Only the Notary may properly write on the certificate portion of a notarized document.

A certificate with the handwriting of more than one person may raise suspicions of tampering. ■

5 Documents Sent Abroad

Some documents sent to other countries may require proof that the Notary's signature and seal are genuine and that the Notary had authority to act at the time of notarization.

More than 90 nations, including the United States, subscribe to the *Hague Convention Abolishing the Requirement of Legalization for Foreign Public Documents.* Under the *Hague Convention*, only one authentication certificate, an *apostille*, is needed to verify the Notary seal on a document sent to another nation.

The rest of the nations have opted to rely on the traditional chain-certification method of authentication, which can require five or more separate certificates, each verifying the previous one.

For more information on the Hague treaty and authentication, visit http://www.hcch.net/index_en.php. ■

ATTORNEY IN FACT

BLIND SIGNERS

6 Signs Own Name

Statutes authorize an attorney in fact to sign the name of another person (the principal signer) on legal documents; however, the attorney in fact also signs his or her own name on the same document.

Here's how the two signatures might appear:

> Mary Q. Smith,
> attorney in fact for
> John P. Smith, principal.

The attorney in fact need not be a lawyer. Indeed, the typical attorney in fact is a nonlawyer who is the spouse or business associate of the principal. ■

7 Read the Document

Before notarizing the signature of a blind person, be sure the individual knows exactly what he or she is signing.

Ask the sightless person to tell you the document's title (or type) and its general purpose. If there is any uncertainty, you may have to read the document aloud to the signer. As a matter of fact, several states, including Florida, Illinois and Indiana, require Notaries to read the document to any blind signer. ■

BONDS

8 Protects the Public

In states that require Notaries to be bonded, a bond protects the public, not the Notary.

Up to a specified amount (ranging from $500 to $15,000) the bond reimburses any person for financial losses caused by a Notary's mistake or misconduct, if the Notary cannot pay. However, once such funds are paid out to a victim, the bonding company will seek to recover the money from the Notary — and will go to great lengths to do so.

The Notary's dual protection from honest mistakes is, first, errors and omissions insurance, which is not mandatory in any state, and, second, a detailed journal of notarial acts, which, by describing all IDs relied on, shows the Notary's reasonable care. ■

9 May Not Be Cancelled

Often when a Notary leaves an employer who has paid for that Notary's commission and bond, the employer will try to "cancel" the bond, mistakenly thinking that liability for the Notary's acts will otherwise continue, or in an effort to recover part of the cost of the bond.

However, neither the Notary nor the employer can cancel a surety bond. As a protection for the public, law requires the bond to remain in effect for the full term of the Notary's commission.

Employers should know that the bond has no effect on their liability for a current or former employee's notarial acts; what does have an effect on liability is whether the employer required improper conduct.

If an employer asks a departing Notary for pro-rated reimbursement for having paid the bond premium, the Notary should be aware that he or she is under no obligation to reimburse, especially if the Notary was directed to get the commission as part of the job. ■

Capacity of Signer

10 Proof Of Capacity

Oftentimes, representatives of small companies are asked to sign papers for their organization but possess no proof of their capacity as a representative.

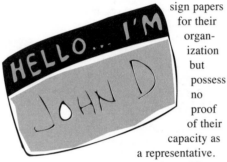

If the Notary's certificate makes no reference to or certification of the signer as a representative, the signer can write "John Doe, Agent" or anything else after the signature without the Notary requiring proof. ■

Certificates

11 Pen vs. Typewriter

Is it best to hand print or to type in the wording on a Notary certificate?

For writing on any legal form, legibility and permanence are critical. A typewriter probably has the edge over hand printing in legibility, but the ink affixed by a pen (especially a fountain pen) is usually more difficult to remove than that affixed by a typewriter.

All things considered, it is probably best to fill out a certificate by hand, printing legibly with a fountain pen filled with black ink. This also provides a document examiner with ample samples of the Notary's writing, in case the genuineness of the certificate is later challenged. ■

12 Confusing Terms

Many terms used in Notary certificates or in documents presented for notarization may seem legalistic and complicated when they actually have a simple or familiar meaning. Here are a few examples:

Affiant .... Affidavit Signer
Attest .... Certify
Depose............................ Swear
Execute .... Sign
Executing   Subscribing
  Witness....................... Witness
Instrument .... Document
Legalize .... Authenticate
Subscribe .... Sign
Verification
  Upon Oath..................... Jurat ■

13 When To Complete

Many Notaries use their own personal "ceremony" when completing a notarization, and while the order in which the separate tasks of a notarization are not typically specified, you should always complete the certificate last.

The certificate details everything that you and the signer did during the notarization, so the identification, oaths/affirmations, signatures on the document, etc. must all have been taken care of before the certificate is completed.

Furthermore, since the notarized document is often the only thing the signer needs, you should ensure that you have collected a fee and completed the journal entry before providing the signer with his or her needs. ■

14 New Notarization

If you are asked to perform a second notarization on a document that has been revised, and to "just send a new acknowledgment certificate with your stamp and signature on it," you must refuse.

You should never send anyone a completed acknowledgment certificate by itself because it could be attached to an unauthorized document. When "reac-knowledging," the document must be returned to you for a brand new notarization. This means that all signers must reappear to acknowledge that they are aware of the changes. (They don't necessarily have to re-sign.) You must complete and attach a new notarial certificate. In states where a Notary journal is required, you also must complete a new entry. ■

15 Out-Of-State Certificates

Beware of blustering, browbeating, out-of-state attorneys who insist that you use Notary forms from their own states, even when these forms aren't in compliance with certificates your state requires you to use. No one — even a person with a law degree — has a right to demand that you disobey your own state laws.

If your state requires a particular type of notarial certificate you may only use an out-of-state Notary form if it is substantially the same.

The out-of-state form doesn't have to be verbatim with the form your state requires (unless the law specifies that it be verbatim), but it must contain the same basic elements.

If you have any doubt that the out-of-state form is substantially the same, use the certificate for your state — and don't feel guilty! ■

16 Prevent Misuse Of Loose Forms

When stapling a "loose" Notary certificate to a document, it's smart to take a few precautions to prevent its removal and fraudulent reattachment.

In the certificate's margin, write a brief description of the document, such as, "This certificate is attached to grant deed dated 7-11-10 and cosigned by Mary Smith." (The NNA's "pre-printed Notary Certificates" provide spaces for this information.)

If you have an embosser seal, either mandatory or optional, you might emboss the certificate and document together, then make a note in your journal that this was done. ■

17 "Hybrid" Certificates

Some notarizations are neither fish nor fowl. A notarial certificate, for example, may combine both acknowledgment and jurat wording, and require the signer both to acknowledge a signature and take an oath from the Notary. Don't be fazed. There are many such "hybrid" notarial acts.

You may describe such a notarization in your journal as "acknowledgment/jurat" or "acknowledgment with oath" or the like. ■

18 Acknowledgment Versus Jurat

While a Notary may not decide on his or her own whether a particular document requires a jurat or an acknowledgment, nothing prevents the Notary from explaining the basic differences between the two notarial acts so that a signer can make the determination.

"For a jurat, I have to watch you sign and give you an oath," you might say. "For an acknowledgment, I have to positively identify you and hear you say that the signature is yours and willingly made. Now, which type of notarization do you want?"

If the signer still doesn't know, he or she should be referred to the person or agency that indicated the notarization was necessary. ■

19 "SS" Is Not Social Security

Contrary to what some Notaries and clients believe, the "SS." that often appears in the venue portion of the notarial certificate is not a space for one's Social Security number.

The letters, which also appear as "SCT.", are actually abbreviations of the Latin word *scilicet*, meaning "namely" or "in particular."

Although the letters have appeared on Notary certificates for centuries, the absence of these two or three letters in the venue does not affect the validity of the certificate. ■

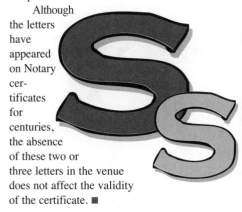

COMMISSION EXPIRATION

20 Impersonation Is A Crime

It is a criminal act to impersonate a Notary, punishable by a fine, imprisonment or both.

Notaries who fail to observe their commission expiration dates may be subject to these stiff criminal penalties, especially if the failure was intentional.

If, for example, you are a Tennessee Notary and your commission expires at midnight on June 7 and you notarize on June 8 or beyond, you may be guilty of a Class C misdemeanor. ■

21 If You Resign

If you decide to resign your Notary commission, notify the secretary of state (or other commissioning authority in your state) in writing and by certified or registered mail if possible, indicating an effective date of resignation.

Surrender any official recordbooks to the office specified by law, and if state law does not prescribe rules for disposing of your official seal, deface or destroy it so that it cannot be misused. Do not leave the journal or seal with an employer.

If you move from the state that commissioned you, you normally must resign your commission — although a few states will allow you to keep it if you continue to work in the state. ■

22 Notarization After Expiration

What should you do if you inadvertently notarize after commission expiration?

First, inform all signers for whom you "notarized." (Yet another reason for recording the name and address for each signer in a journal of notarial acts.) Since you weren't officially a Notary, signers of certain sensitive and important documents like wills and property deeds may rush to get these papers properly notarized. In the case of other documents, there may be less urgency or need to do so.

Some states have so-called "curative" laws that recognize the validity of imperfect notarizations performed in good faith if these acts aren't challenged within a certain time period, typically one year from the date of notarization. These laws may apply to notarizations performed with an expired commission. ■

COMMISSION JURISDICTION

23 Commissioned By One State

It's legally possible to be a Notary in more than one state at the same time.

A growing number of states, for example, allow out-of-state residents to apply for Notary commissions if they work or maintain an office in another state. Thus, a New Jersey resident who commutes to work in New York City every day may qualify for a New York State Notary commission; that same person, of course, could also qualify for a New Jersey commission. But the New Jersey commission, seal and rules could only be used in New Jersey, and the New York commission, seal and rules only in New York.

A Notary declaring residence in two or more states normally may not qualify for a Notary commission in both or all states simultaneously. Why? Because a Notary commission applicant must declare a state of *primary* residence and that is the only state that will then issue a commission. The state of primary residence normally is where one is registered to vote, holds a driver's license, and pays state income taxes. ■

24 Commission Is Not Transferable

Although it would be convenient, your Notary commission is not transferable from one state to another.

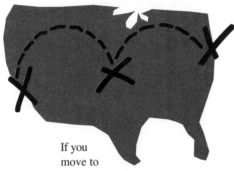

If you move to a new state, you must "start from square one" in applying for a new Notary commission.

A few states will even make you wait before you can apply. Montana, for instance, imposes a one-year residency requirement.

Before moving to a new state, don't forget to surrender your Notary journal (if one must be kept) to the appropriate public office, and to either surrender your seal as law requires or destroy or deface it so it can't be misused. ■

25 Powers Differ By State

Other states and nations don't set the rules that govern you as a Notary — only the state that commissioned you does.

Irritatingly, though, out-of-state and foreign visitors will sometimes ask you to perform notarial acts that may be legal for Notaries in their native jurisdictions but not in yours.

A transplanted Floridian, for instance, might insist that you can perform a marriage because, "Notaries in Florida do marriages all the time." Or a Latino immigrant might swear that you have authority to certify his birth certificate because, "Any *Notario* in Guadalajara could do it."

What makes such requests confounding is that the individuals are so often convinced they are right and you are wrong that they become angry.

All you can do is tactfully and patiently explain that the powers of Notaries differ radically from state to state and nation to nation. ■

COMMISSIONING PROCESS

26 File Bond First

In most states, newly commissioned Notaries must file their oaths of office (and bond, if applicable) within a specific period of time, or the commission becomes void automatically. In New Jersey, for example, filing must be completed within three months.

Smart Notaries will never notarize before filing their oath and bond.

Why? Because even though the new Notary may have the best intentions, unforeseen circumstances such as illness or even simple forgetfulness may cause him or her to miss the filing deadline. An unpleasant result could be that any notarizations performed with the now-voided commission would have to be re-done, lest they be challenged as invalid. ■

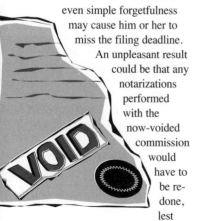

27 Not Eligible

A single past conviction for a crime does not necessarily mean an applicant cannot become a Notary, especially if there have been many years of exemplary conduct since the conviction.

It is unlikely, for example, that a one-time conviction for drunk driving or for disturbing the peace would permanently prevent issuance of a Notary commission.

However, any person with multiple felony convictions or with even a single conviction for a crime of dishonesty — forgery, counterfeiting, fraud — has little chance of ever receiving a Notary commission. ■

COPY CERTIFICATIONS

28 Official Certifiers

Anyone can "certify" a copy of a personally kept paper by attaching a personally signed statement that it is identical to the original.

Corporations and private institutions can certify copies of

their papers by attaching a signed statement from an authorized employee and using the organizational seal or letterhead.

However, only Notaries, county recorders, custodians of vital records, and certain other public officers may officially certify copies as agents of the government. ■

CREDIBLE WITNESS

29 A Walking, Talking ID

A Notary may identify a stranger either through ID cards or the word of a reliable person, a "credible witness," who is personally known by the Notary. This witness must swear (or affirm) to the Notary that he/she personally knows the signer and has the identity claimed.

Since the word of a credible witness or witnesses is regarded as satisfactory evidence of identity and equivalent to a photo ID, many Notaries think of a credible witness as a "walking, talking ID card." ■

DATES

30 Postdated Documents

You're just about to notarize a document when

you realize that the date below the signer's signature is several days later than today's date.

The signing date on a document should always precede or coincide with the date of notarization. If you notice a discrepancy, you should point it out to the signer, since a document dated later than the notarial certificate could be questioned or even rejected by a recorder wondering how a document could have been signed *after* it was notarized. ■

DEEDS

EDUCATION

31 Use Caution With Deeds

Bonding companies report that well over two-thirds of the lawsuits targeting Notaries involve real estate deeds.

If Notaries would make it a point to double their caution in notarizing real property deeds, the nation would see a significant decrease in forged, coerced and incompetent signings — and the often reported "gridlock" in the court system would ease.

Just imagine that you see the words "Proceed Carefully" at the top of every deed you notarize. Then, take special pains to identify each signer and to make sure that the signer appears to be aware of the importance of the document. ■

32 Often Not Required

Too many Notaries are appallingly ignorant of the vital precepts and practices of notarization. A frightening number aren't aware that:

• The document signer (or subscribing witness) must always appear face to face before the Notary at the time of notarization.

• State law must always take precedence over the dictates of an employer.

• A signer should not be identified based on an unsworn, informal introduction by a third party.

• A Social Security card or a birth certificate is worthless as an identifying document.

• Notaries should not "lend out" their seals. ■

EMBOSSERS

33 Old Tool Is Still Effective

Modern office printers and copying machines that can duplicate any inked seal are reviving the importance of the old-fashioned

Notary embosser. The centuries-old Notary tool can deter fraud by identifying original documents through its three-dimensional impression. If your state law only requires use of an inking seal, adding an embossment will provide greater insurance against any fraudulent reproduction of the document.

On a multi-page document, a single embossment through all the pages can make fraudulent replacement of any one page — or of the Notary's attached certificate — nearly impossible. A forger would not only have to create a new phony page, but also exactly duplicate the embosser's impression. ■

EMPLOYER

34 It's Your Commission

Just because your private employer paid for your Notary commission, bond, seal, journal and notarial supplies, doesn't mean you can't use this commission on your own time.

The commission belongs to you, not your employer, and you may notarize in the evenings and during weekends — even during vacations, as long as you stay in the state in which you are commissioned.

Your employer can't legally demand that you keep the seal and journal in the company office outside business hours. The seal and journal are official adjuncts of the public office of Notary and they belong to you, regardless of who paid for them. ■

E & O INSURANCE

FEES

35 When Does E&O Apply?

Suppose you're sued for a notarization you performed five years ago; you had Notary errors and omissions insurance at the time, but the policy expired four years ago.

Will you be covered by that "E&O" policy for today's lawsuit?

With most policies, you will be. The typical E&O policy (called an "occurrence policy") covers notarial acts occurring any time during the policy term, even when a lawsuit is filed well after the policy term expires.

As long as you had a valid Notary commission at the time and did not purposely break the law when you notarized, you should be covered.

Be sure to keep and safeguard your Notary E&O policy after its expiration date. The NNA recommends keeping it for 10 years. ■

36 Agree To Fees In Advance

If you charge mileage or a travel fee for driving to perform a notarization, you should ensure that your client understands and agrees to all fees before you even get in the car. (We're talking about the majority of the states whose laws don't prescribe a mileage fee for Notaries.)

Over the telephone, you should carefully explain that the mileage or travel fee is a mutually agreed upon private charge that is entirely separate from the fee allowed by statute for a notarial act.

Once your client agrees upon a mileage or travel fee and understands that it is neither required nor specified by law and will be imposed in addition to the regular fee for a notarial act, you may then get in your car. ■

37 Fees Not Required

Just because state law entitles you to charge a specified maximum amount for notarizing a signature (e.g., 50 cents, $1, or $10 per signature) doesn't mean you can't charge *less* than that amount — or charge nothing at all!

In fact, persons requesting notarization of dozens or even hundreds of documents at once may shop around for the

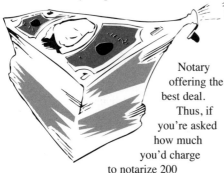

Notary offering the best deal. Thus, if you're asked how much you'd charge to notarize 200 documents for a condominium association, you may be entitled to charge a total of $1,000 if your state permits a $5-per signature fee. However, your chances of actually getting the job might be better if you offer to do it for $400, or $2 per signature. ■

FEMALE SIGNERS

38 'Feme Covert'

Ever notice those occasional strange provisions in state codes that say, "An acknowledgment of a married woman may be made in the same form as though she were unmarried"?

These are holdovers from a sexist era, surprisingly not so long ago, when a married woman was assumed to be under the physical and intellectual domination of her husband (a legal concept known as *feme covert*).

In those days, a Notary by law had to question a married woman out of the presence of her husband to ensure there was no undue influence; but as women won the right to vote (1920) and were recognized under law as men's equals, the states removed these protective warnings from statute — though a few still survive. ■

FINGERPRINTS

39 Protection Against Forgery

In the battle against forgers and impostors, requesting a journal fingerprint is the Notary's best weapon of defense. No impostor wants to leave behind irrefutable evidence linking him or her to a forgery.

When asked to leave a fingerprint, the impostor may raise his voice in protest, bluster about an invasion of privacy or back away, claiming he suddenly remembered leaving the dog in the car with the windows closed, never to be seen again.

In all states except California, however, the Notary is empowered only to *ask* that a print be left; he or she cannot insist. Yet the request alone can be enough to thwart an impostor. ■

40 ID Still Required

If you fingerprint as a business sideline, take at least as much care in identifying the persons you fingerprint as in identifying the persons for whom you notarize.

U.S. Citizenship and Immigration Services (USCIS) has reported a growing problem with fingerprint cards submitted by individuals applying for citizenship who cover up a criminal record by using another person's prints. This can easily be done because many private fingerprinting agencies don't ask for identification. ■

FOREIGN SIGNERS

41 Communicating With Signer

A Notary must communicate directly with a document signer in order to make accurate and uninfluenced judgments about the signer's identity, willingness and awareness.

Communicating with the

signer through a translator or interpreter can lead to problems: a dishonest translator may misrepresent the document to the signer.

The Notary should always communicate with the signer in the same language, whether this language be English, Spanish, Chinese, Farsi or even sign language. ■

43 Try A Consulate

If an American traveling or visiting abroad needs a signature notarized on a document that is to be sent back to the United States, this person should stop by the nearest U.S. consulate, since consular officials have notarial powers. Visiting a foreign Notary for a simple jurat or acknowledgment should generally be avoided. The services of foreign Notaries will be more expensive, and getting their seals and signatures authenticated to facilitate acceptance in the United States can be time-consuming. ■

42 Non-U.S. Citizens

Some Notaries believe they need only serve document signers who are U.S. citizens.

They are sorely mistaken.

Any member of the general public, citizen or foreigner, who needs a lawful notarization performed must not be turned away.

Notaries exist in every country, and they are relied on by the foreign visitor to help process paperwork that is often critically important in their lives.

Notaries turning away foreigners in large numbers would have an adverse impact on international relations.

Only when an illegal or unauthorized notarial act is requested is a Notary justified in refusing to serve a non-native. ■

44 Passport Card

Effective June 1, 2009, a wallet-size U.S. "Passport Card" allows land and sea travel between this nation and Canada, Mexico, the Caribbean region, and Bermuda. The card may not be used for air travel — only a traditional U.S. passport book may be used for this purpose.

The passport card is designed to serve the needs of resident communities on our northern and southern borders. It is not a globally accepted travel document, as is the passport book.

The card is a result of the Intelligence Reform and Terrorism Presentation Act of 2004, requiring all travelers to present a passport or other document that denotes identity and citizenship when entering the United States. ■

45 Kids Abroad

Parents allowing children to travel abroad with a relative or friend may need to have their signatures notarized on an authorization letter.

A child visiting Mexico escorted by persons other than his or her parents, for example, may need a detailed letter of consent (mentioning dates and itinerary) bearing the notarized signatures of both parents, in addition to normal travel documents. If asked about a particular nation's requirements or what format a parental consent letter should take, refer the questioner to the consulate of the given country for a definitive answer. ■

IDENTIFICATION OF SIGNER

46 Acceptable IDs

California, Florida and Tennessee were the first states to

stipulate exactly what IDs a Notary may use to identify a signer. The allowed IDs include state driver's licenses and official non-driver's IDs, U.S. and foreign passports, and U.S. military IDs. The three generally specify that any ID must contain a photo, physical description, signature and identifying number, and must be current or have been issued within the past five years.

These are excellent ID guidelines for Notaries in *any* state. ■

47 Name on ID Must Match

With ID cards, the Notary can follow the less-but-not-more policy. If an ID card presented by a signer reads "John Albert Smith," the Notary may accept the signature "John Smith," "John A. Smith," or "J. Smith." The Notary, however, cannot accept more than what appears on the ID. For example, the Notary couldn't write "John Albert Smith" on the notarial certificate if the ID only read "John A. Smith." ■

48 Photos Can't Be Identical

What does it mean when you see exactly the same photograph on all the ID cards presented to you by a document signer?

Or, if the clothes and background in the ID photos are exactly the same in all of the photos?

It probably means you're looking at counterfeit or tampered identification documents, because ID-issuing agencies do not share photos. And it's highly unlikely the signer would have worn exactly the same clothes and stood in front of exactly the same background during different photo shoots.

Such improbable similarities are a "red flag" that should prompt you to examine the cards closely and to question their bearer even more carefully. ■

49 Only One ID Required

How many ID cards are needed to positively identify a signer who is a stranger to the Notary?

One good card may suffice, if there are no suspicious circumstances. By itself, a government-issued, photo-bearing ID such as a state driver's license or a U.S. passport can reliably identify a stranger. Of course, if there is any solid evidence that the card has been tampered with (e.g., new photo has been pasted over original photo), the Notary should decline the notarization.

Further, even if the card looks good, any suspicious circumstances (such as the cardholder's unfamiliarity with the birthdate or address on the card) should cause the Notary to question the validity of the ID.

It never hurts to ask for more than one ID, even if that second card is a Social Security card, student ID or other document that might never by itself be convincing proof of identity. ■

50 Chain, Chain, Chain

When you rely on a credible witness to identify a document signer who is a stranger, there must be a chain of personal knowledge from you, the Notary, to the credible witness to the signer.

In other words, you must personally know the witness and the witness must personally know the signer. You should not identify the witness using ID cards.

Some states may also allow a Notary to use two credible witnesses whom the Notary does not personally know, as long as those witnesses also provide acceptable ID. ■

IMMIGRATION DOCUMENTS

51 Seal Still Required

The immigration document most often notarized is the "Affidavit of Support," requiring the Notary to complete jurat wording.

The Affidavit of Support is signed by a person promising to financially support an immigrant while present in the United States.

Like most documents issued by the United States Citizenship and Immigration Services (USCIS), the Affidavit is tightly crammed with wording, leaving little room to affix a Notary seal. Even so, USCIS officials stress that a seal, if required by state law, must be affixed somewhere on the Affidavit. It should be positioned to cover minimal wording — ideally, over "boilerplate" wording — and never over signatures, typing or hand printing.

Almost all USCIS documents requiring notarization bear jurats for the Notary to complete. ■

52 Immigration Assistance

You're kicked back in your chair, relaxing after a day of relatively simple notarizations. The clock is inching toward five when your last client approaches and asks if you can help him prepare immigration papers. You pause, trying to remember the rule — can you help or not?

It all depends on what is meant by "help." A nonattorney can offer clerical, secretarial or translating services to a person preparing immigration papers, as long as no counseling on immigration issues is offered.

Only an attorney or trained USCIS representative can offer advice. ■

IMPARTIALITY

53 Employee Notaries

Corporate employee Notaries may notarize documents for the corporation, unless named as a party to a particular transaction either individually or as a representative. Many states even allow stockholders, directors and officers of the corporation to notarize with the same limitations. To preserve impartiality, however, it is always best if the notarizing corporate employee, stockholder, director or officer is strictly salaried and does not stand to gain financially from the transaction requiring a notarial act. ∎

54 Attorney-Notary Exception

What's up with attorney-Notaries? Can they notarize for clients?

It depends on state law. California and Florida, for example, give attorneys special privileges to notarize for clients without regarding their fees as a disqualifying interest. Oklahoma allows attorneys to notarize for clients as long as the document will not be filed in a case involving that client. Other states have different rules.

Because the role of the Notary as impartial witness and the role of the attorney as advocate are in basic conflict, it is always safest for the attorney to find an uninvolved Notary to notarize for a client, regardless of state law. ∎

JOURNAL

55 Reasonable Care

For Notaries in our litigious society, there is no absolute defense against being sued. There is, however, an all but airtight defense against being found liable in court: reasonable care, the degree of care used by that theoretical "normal" person.

Notaries who can clearly show they used reasonable care in performing a notarial act may not be found liable.

Reasonable care means obeying every law (e.g., never notarize without the signer present) and operating cautiously at all times. It also means keeping a detailed journal of notarial acts that describes how each signer was identified — whether or not a journal is required by law. ∎

56 Additional Information

Your journal should be as complete a record of your notarial acts as possible. In addition to entry spaces for date and time, type of notarial act, type of document, principals' signature and how the signer was identified, most Notary journals also have a column for "Additional Pertinent Information," or the like. What is included in this space?

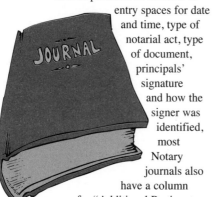

Add any particulars about the notarization that are not covered by the other spaces, such as where the act took place if not at the Notary's office, who was present, the number of pages in the document and whether a "loose" certificate was attached.

It's also a good idea to include descriptions of the signer's behavior if it seems suspicious (e.g., "Signer appeared extremely nervous.") Be accurate, because everything you write down could be important if your journal is ever called into court as evidence in a lawsuit. ■

57 Multiple Journals

Keeping and using more than one Notary journal and seal at the same time is a bad idea.

It can be difficult enough keeping track of just one journal and seal. If there were two, you'd only be increasing the possibility of these items being lost, stolen or used without your knowledge.

Also, each journal would give an incomplete picture of all the notarial acts you performed over a given period of time, since some acts would be recorded in one journal and the rest in the other.

A journal should be complete in itself and provide a full, chronological accounting of official activities during your commission terms. ■

58 Lost Journal And Seal

You lost the sofa in a mudslide, found your family photos two towns away after a flood, your personal computer hasn't bounced back from an earthquake and you can't find your official seal or records. What would you do if you lost these two vital notarial tools in a natural disaster?

Notify in writing the office where the records (and possibly the seal) would have been deposited. Return receipt requested. Keep the receipt.

Buy a new recordbook and seal, noting in the front of the journal what happened to the old records. Be sure to order a seal that is noticeably different from the old one to point out any unauthorized use of the missing seal. ∎

59 Files Can't Replace Journal

An office filing system is no substitute for a bound journal of notarial acts.

The entries in a journal, which should fully describe each notarization and include the signature of each document signer, can be safeguarded by the Notary in a locked drawer; and the chronological listing of notarial acts on numbered, bound pages can reveal attempts to remove or tamper with entries.

As protection both for the public and themselves, all Notaries should keep bound recordbooks of their notarial acts, even when not required to do so by state law. And these important journals should be locked away when not in use.

Keeping file copies of notarized documents or of miscellaneous loose notes pertaining to a notarization does not constitute a reliable and secure record system. ∎

60 Journal Aids Memory

Courtroom trials caused by a Notary's alleged misconduct typically occur from two to five years after the contested notarization.

Years after the fact, a Notary normally cannot testify accurately in court about the critical particulars of a notarial act without a recordbook to jog the memory.

How can you prove to a judge or a jury that you used the required degree of care in identifying a signer unless you have a journal entry showing the serial numbers of the IDs you relied on?

Keep a journal of notarial acts for your own protection. ∎

61 Protect Journal Information

Even though your journal of notarial acts is a public record, you should regard the information recorded therein as sensitive and confidential.

Always ask anyone interested in examining an entry to be specific about what they want to see. Do not allow aimless "fishing expeditions" through the journal, and never surrender control of this

important record to anyone.

People often have intensely personal papers notarized. It would be a serious breach of the trust placed in you, as a public official, to disclose facts entered in your journal to anyone unless the inquirer makes a formal request in writing, identifies himself or herself, and provides specifics about the act or acts sought.

When providing a photocopy of a journal entry, cover up other entries on the page. ∎

62 Don't Keep Document Copies

Incredibly, many Notaries keep copies of every document they notarize.

Why incredible?

Because they're able to convince every document signer that leaving behind a copy of what may be a quite sensitive and personal paper is a requirement of law. It's not.

Only in certifying a copy might a Notary be justified in keeping a backup copy as a notarial record.

As long as you maintain a detailed and accurate journal of notarial acts, it isn't necessary to keep copies of the documents you notarize. Indeed, document signers would be rightfully outraged at any Notary who wants to keep a copy of a personal document because the Notary may be too lazy to maintain a journal. ∎

63 Separate Entries

We've all been there: a signer stops by (sometimes, it's your boss), and asks you to perform a dozen notarizations on very similar documents. Though tempting, a Notary should never include more than one notarization per journal entry.

Some states specifically prohibit doing so, and while

many states don't address recording multiple notarizations in a single entry at all, the very concept of keeping a sequential journal of all notarial acts does not allow it. If you were to simply "check off" that you notarized 10 deeds in your journal entry, and the signer signed only one time, the record is all but useless.

Years later, the deed could be contested in court, and a simple, "I don't remember signing that," could let someone escape his or her obligation to pay back a debt. ■

Jurats

64 Term Misused

Be aware that the term "jurat" is still widely misused.

Many people, even lawyers, apply this term to any and every Notary certificate, even to acknowledgment forms.

Correctly used, "jurat" only applies to the wording "Subscribed and Sworn (or affirmed) before me this _____ day of _____, 20___, by _____,"

or similar wording, found in affidavits, depositions or other written, sworn statements. ■

65 Include Signers' Names

You may have noticed that the wording of most jurat certificates is somewhat indefinite: "Subscribed and sworn to (or affirmed) before me this _____ day of _____, 20___."

Subscribed and sworn to by whom? One person? Ten? A hundred?

The number of signatures that appear on the document is not a reliable indicator of how many signers actually appeared before the Notary because signatures can be fraudulently 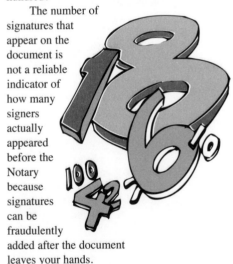 added after the document leaves your hands.

A smart Notary will therefore add and complete the short phrase "...by (name of signer[s])" at the end of the jurat, right after the year. ■

66 Leave It Alone

The wording, "Subscribed and sworn to before me by ___ on this ___ day of ___, 20 ___" constitutes a typical jurat and, when appearing with a statement of venue ("State of ___, County of ___"), is a full-fledged Notary certificate. No other certificate wording is needed.

Yet, believing that more than this brief wording is necessary, many Notaries want to also attach an acknowledgment certificate.

Acknowledgments and jurats are very different forms of notarization. Just leave that jurat alone — it's all you need! ■

MINORS

67 Identifying A Minor

Can a child serve as a credible witness? Generally the answer is no, even though state laws rarely specify qualifications other than that a credible witness be personally known to the Notary. (In California, even a personally known credible witness must present identification.) A credible witness must be mature enough to understand the term "personally known." Most children below the teen years can't be expected to have such judgment.

Nonetheless, courts of law may, on occasion, recognize a child as a credible witness whose testimony can be taken as evidence.

Whenever possible, a Notary should rely on a personally known adult (an individual at least 18 or 21 years old, depending on state law) to serve as a credible witness. If the witness is ever to be under 18 years old, he or she should only be an unusually mature and reliable person in his or her late teens. ■

MISCONDUCT/ PUNISHMENT

68 False Information

In every state, it is a criminal act — either a misdemeanor or a felony — for a Notary or other public official to intentionally fill out a false certificate.

It is also a crime to falsify a date, state that a person appeared before you at the time of notarization when he or she did not, and to state that you personally know a signer when you do not.

Remember this the next time you are pressured to "fudge" when completing an acknowledgment or jurat form.

Around the world, great faith is put in the truthfulness of a Notary's certificate. This is the reason the penalties for falsehood are so severe. ■

69 Reporting Misconduct

If you know of a Notary who makes a habit of performing his or her official acts negligently or illegally, you should consider it your public duty to report that individual to the state Notary-regulating office. Reports can be made anonymously.

Notaries are commissioned to protect the public interest, not violate it. Just like bad police officers, bad Notaries must be weeded out at every possible opportunity. One negligent or dishonest Notary discredits all Notaries. ■

70 Penalties

Certain intentional violations by a Notary may result in three separate kinds of punishment at the same time. Suppose, for example, a Notary knowingly signs and seals a false certificate stating a signer appeared when in fact he or she did not.

First, the Notary may be criminally

*PROSECUTION
*CIVIL LAWSUIT
*COMMISSION
 REVOCATION

prosecuted for making a false official certificate and/or for criminal conspiracy to defraud.

The penalties: fines and/or imprisonment.

Second, the Notary may be targeted by a civil lawsuit seeking to recover funds lost by a private citizen as a result of the Notary's illegal actions. The penalty: possible loss of all personal assets.

And third, the Notary's commission may be revoked. The hidden penalty: the unlikelihood that the Notary will ever again qualify for a commission or license of any kind (real estate, insurance, etc.).

Always obey the law, particularly the law requiring every signer to appear before you at the time of notarization. ■

NOTARIZING FOR RELATIVES

71 Spouses

It's never a good idea to notarize for your spouse, for two reasons.

First, the financial and personal affairs of a husband and wife are usually so intertwined that the Notary risks violating the state laws prohibiting a financial or beneficial interest.

Second, a document notarized by the spouse of the signer is more likely to be challenged in a court of law. Why? Because the Notary has forfeited his or her essential impartiality, and it more readily may be argued that the document should be voided due to undue influence — either by the Notary on the signer, or by the signer on the Notary. ■

OATHS/ AFFIRMATIONS

72 Don't Forget To Give Oath

Either out of carelessness or apathy, too many Notaries fail to administer legally required oaths to affiants (signers of affidavits), deponents and witnesses.

There has been a surprising number of civil and criminal cases thrown out of the court because a Notary failed to give an oath to a signer.

Certain testimony can't be used as evidence in court unless the testifier is under oath. Failure to give an oath within a specified time may disqualify critical evidence.

In most cases, the oath wording is left up to the Notary to create, but such wording should always contain the phrase, "Do you solemnly swear (or affirm) that…." The oath-taker must answer aloud, or in writing if he or she cannot speak. ■

73 Depositions

Though many states empower all their Notaries to take depositions, only Notaries who are shorthand reporters qualified on a stenotype machine normally have the skills to do so.

However, Notaries without such stenographic talents are sometimes asked to *help* take a deposition. The reason: the shorthand reporter in attendance does not have a Notary commission, or is from another state, and cannot therefore swear in the deponent or execute the required jurat. ■

PERSONAL APPEARANCE

74 Phone Call Isn't Personal Appearance

Why is it illegal to take an acknowledgment over the telephone?

First, because neither the Notary nor the caller can be absolutely sure that the document in the Notary's possession is the exact document the caller wants to acknowledge.

Second, because identity, awareness and willingness to sign cannot be definitively determined by the Notary without the face-to-face presence of the signer. Without the Notary's knowledge, for example, a signer could be making a phone call under duress of physical threat by a silent party. ■

75 Working With Bosses

Once again your boss asks you to notarize the signature of an absent spouse or an absent client.

A sticky situation, but, as always, you must never comply. It's a criminal act for a Notary to sign a certificate stating that an individual was present when in fact the person was not.

Some bosses are savvy enough not to make such requests. Others may need to be educated. Articles copied from the pages of NNA publications have proven extremely helpful in educating many an employer. Remember, though, that when dealing with your boss, the most helpful tool of all is tact. ■

READING THE DOCUMENT

76 Don't Scrutinize Documents

You needn't read any document you notarize, other than to note its title, date and the name of its signer and to scan for blank spaces. You aren't expected to check for inaccurate or fraudulent statements.

However, should you happen to

know or note that any document or transaction is deceptive, false or fraudulent, you are obliged to withhold your notarial services — and report any unlawful activity to the police or to your Notary-regulating office.

Remember though, you are expected to carefully read and heed every word in the notarial certificates you fill out — you will be held personally responsible for their accuracy and truthfulness. ■

This is wrong. Notaries must always follow their own state laws. According to Article IV, Section 1, of the U.S. Constitution, each state must recognize the official acts of all other states.

The lawful seal, certificates and procedures used by a Notary in one state cannot be rejected as unlawful simply because they do not comply with statutes in another state. ■

SEALS

77 Follow Your State's Laws

Notarizing documents that "travel" between states is becoming more and more common. So is the posing of questions like: "I'm notarizing a document that will be sent to (name of state). Can you tell me whether that state requires an inking or embossing seal?"

This question is based on the assumption that Notaries in one state must follow the rules of the document's destination state when notarizing.

78 Disposal of Seal

When your Notary commission is expired, resigned or revoked, you must properly dispose of your official seal to prevent its misuse.

But only a few states set procedures for disposal of a seal. In Oregon, for example, a Notary with a revoked commission must deliver the seal to the secretary of state within 30 days and, if the commission just expires normally, the Oregon Notary must destroy the seal as soon as possible.

Most other states don't have such specific rules.

In the absence of official procedures for disposing of a seal, the ex-Notary should destroy or deface the seal's printing face. A hammer can readily deface the soft metal in an embosser die, while a knife or scissors can usually do the job with a rubber or plastic inking stamp. ■

79 Color of Ink

Black is widely regarded as the best ink color to use in affixing an official Notary signature or seal, because it is easy to microfilm legibly. Exceptions: Utah requires that a Notary seal be affixed in purple ink so that photocopies of the notarized document can readily be distinguished from the original. Tennessee requires the seal to be affixed in any photocopiable color — but not in black or yellow. ■

80 Seal And Embosser

If your state requires you to use a seal, either an inking stamp or an embosser, on every notarized document, is there any reason you can't use <u>two</u> seals, both the inking stamp and the embosser?

No, as long as they aren't affixed over each other, nor over a signature or other writing.

Both types of seal offer an advantage. The inking seal imprints an image that can be readily photocopied, one that recorders are always grateful to see. And the embossing seal can prevent fraudulent replacement of a document page, or of an attached notarial certificate, if the pages and certificate are crimped together. ■

81 When Seal Is Not Required

Notaries in the handful of states whose laws don't require seals may use them anyway. In fact, state officials encourage their use on documents sent out of state, because the absence of a seal often causes a document to be questioned or challenged in states where seals are mandatory.

Although a handful of states don't require Notary seals, in effect they do: there is usually a requirement that the Notary's name, title and commission expiration date be stamped, typed or printed in ink that can be photocopied near the Notary's signature. This is data that appears in the seal in most other states. ■

82 Include Expiration Date

Since most states require the Notary's commission expiration date to be affixed to each document notarized, why not have the date included within the seal, avoiding any possibility of accidental omission? Check your state's Notary handbook because a few states (such as Colorado) specify exactly what must go in the seal. ■

83 Cleaned Your Seal Lately?

Make sure your stamp is clean and free of ink deposits and linty debris that could alter or blur the impression.

To clean the face of an inking stamp, many Notaries merely touch a piece of adhesive tape to the raised letters to remove paper particles or dust.

Note: Never use a sharp-edged instrument to clean your seal — it could damage the letters. Similarly, avoid immersing the stamp in water, since any identifying label may come off. In addition, do not employ a toothbrush or use soap, which can scrape and alter the seal's surface. ■

84 Don't Prestamp Notary Certificates

A Notary's seal should never be prestamped on documents, no matter how many documents that Notary witnesses each day.

Each seal impression should be personally and individually affixed by the Notary, and only at the time of notarization.

Using prestamped certificates makes it easy for the forger. ■

85 Keep Seal Secured

Those two weeks at the beach were great, but you weren't prepared to spend some additional time away from the office — in handcuffs. An unlikely scenario, but it is important to be clear that you are the only individual legally allowed to use your official Notary seal.

Authorizing a supervisor or co-worker to use this device in your absence is foolish and potentially felonious, particularly if your seal is used to perpetrate a fraud.

Lock up your seal and record book before leaving the office, then kick back and really enjoy the summer! ■

86 No Seal Impression

If your office receives a notarized document from another state that doesn't bear a Notary seal, don't automatically assume that the seal was omitted by mistake and the document is invalid.

A number of states don't require Notaries to affix official seals on the documents they notarize — though nothing prevents Notaries in those states from doing so.

Even though a seal may not be mandated in a given state, Notaries may still be required to print, type or stamp such information as their name and commission expiration date. (The NNA's *U.S. Notary Reference Manual* is the best source on all such requirements.) ■

SIGNATURE

87 Signature Guarantee

Signature guarantees are not notarial acts, and anyone performing a signature guarantee must not use the title and seal of a Notary Public when doing so.

Signature guarantees are used by banks and other financial institutions to authenticate signatures on documents related to the transfer of securities. The signature on the document is visually compared with another kept on file.

Notarial acts, on the other hand, are never based on the simple comparison of two signatures — only on careful identification of the signer, who must be face-to-face before the Notary. ■

88 Signature Legibility

Does a signature have to be legible before you can notarize it?

That depends mainly on whether the signature, legible or not, is the same as that appearing on the person's driver's license and other IDs.

If an illegible scrawl is the person's normal signature, and if the signature on the document and marked in the journal matches that on the IDs, then the unreadable signature may be notarized. (Always clearly print the individual's name under or near the journal signature.)

A note of caution: Unscrupulous persons on occasion may write out their signatures illegibly so they can back out of a contract by claiming forgery; and forgers themselves may sign a phony name illegibly to complicate their potential prosecution for fraud.

Always be sure to match the signatures between the documents, IDs and journal. ■

89 When Witnessing A Signature

If someone asks to notarize a document and his signature has already been affixed, that person must sign the document again in your presence.

Why? Because your jurat reads, "Subscribed (this means 'signed') and sworn to before me...." Note the all-important words "before me."

However, if someone asks you to notarize a deed or other document bearing an acknowledgment, it doesn't matter whether the signature has been affixed in or out of your presence. The vital thing is that the signer be present to acknowledge having signed. ■

90 Faxed Signatures

A faxed document may lawfully be notarized only if its signature is affixed by pen and ink after the document comes off

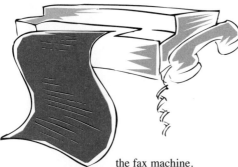

the fax machine.

A glossy-surface faxed document should never be notarized because its printing will fade in time; it is best to first photocopy such a document on bond paper and then sign and notarize the photocopy. A faxed signature, of course, may never be notarized. ■

91 Electronic Signatures Require Physical Presence

Conference calls have become an increasingly common tool that allows corporate teams thousands of miles apart to negotiate, draft and even sign contracts without getting on an airplane or using overnight delivery. The documents are "signed" electronically and some machines can even affix a Notary seal. However, before you decide to notarize a signature on a document 500 miles away, be warned that current state laws don't authorize such "remote notarizations."

Unless the document signer is in your physical presence, you may not truthfully complete a notarial certificate stating that the signer "appeared before you." ■

SIGNATURE BY MARK

92 Proof of Execution Not Acceptable

Can a signature by mark be notarized through a proof of execution by a subscribing witness?

It's not a good idea, since custom (if not state law) has long dictated that the Notary be among the two or three witnesses who watch the signer make the "X." By definition, a subscribing witness appears when the principal signer cannot.

Though it may be inconvenient, it is best that the marker appear in person before a Notary, along with the one or two other witnesses that may be required by state law to identify the marker and watch the mark as it is made. ■

93 Fingerprint May Be Used

Just like an "X," an inked fingerprint may serve as the mark of an illiterate or disabled person, as long as it is properly witnessed and there are no contrary specifications about the format of the mark.

The print should be witnessed by at least two people in addition to the Notary, and one witness would write the print-maker's name beside the print and both witnesses would sign and leave their addresses underneath.

A properly witnessed mark — whether a fingerprint, an "X" or any other symbol — is a legally recognized substitute for a signature. ■

UNAUTHORIZED PRACTICE OF LAW

94 Authorized To Give Advice

Notaries should not decide the type of certificate or notarial act a particular document needs, since this decision can have important legal ramifications. The signer should be asked to find out the required type of notarization from the agency that issued or that will receive the document.

An exception occurs when the Notary's own office is the issuing or receiving agency and the type of document to be notarized is quite familiar to the Notary. In this case, the Notary, wearing the hat of properly trained and experienced employee, might prescribe the type of notarial form that training and experience indicates is appropriate.

All Notaries, however, are allowed some latitude in certificate selection. If, for example, a Notary is asked to notarize a deed bearing an acknowledgment form for an individual when the signer wants to sign as a partner, then that Notary may select and use a partnership acknowledgment form; the basic decision of whether to perform an acknowledgment or a jurat has already been made for the Notary. ■

95 Do Not Offer Advice

If you are a secretary or clerk who types important legal documents for others, you must be careful not to give legal advice nor tell your clients how to word a document.

It is critical to remember that, as a nonattorney, you are prohibited from offering any advice or recommendations to the individual dictating the information. Transcribing the person's words exactly as spoken will protect you from possible prosecution for the unauthorized practice of law. ■

UNDUE INFLUENCE

practice would be to have a Notary outside the deal (such as a salaried secretary in your office) perform the notarization. You are then better protected against possible allegations of high-pressure sales and undue influence. ■

96 Maintain Impartiality

A Notary must never attempt to influence a person to sign or not sign a document requiring a notarial act by that Notary. That would be undue influence and a potential legal reason for invalidating the document.

There is one exception to that rule. If a Notary knows that a transaction is false, fraudulent or illegal, the Notary has an ethical duty to refuse to notarize and, as a responsible public official, may try to influence the parties not to proceed. ■

97 Conflict Of Interest

You've wined and dined the client for months and you've finally got a deal. The only piece of business left is to sign and notarize the documents and deposit that commission check.

But wait a minute — as a Notary you are expected to be an impartial witness. Even though some states will permit notarizing for a sales client, a better business

VENUE

98 Unique Jurisdictions

Placed at the top of a notarial certificate, the venue indicates the state and county (and sometimes the city) in which the notarization occurred. Since Alaska and Louisiana have no counties, the judicial district and parish, respectively, replace the county in the venue for those states.

But Notaries in our nation's capital need not be any more detailed in their venue than "District of Columbia." ■

99 Correcting Venues

The venue portion of the notarial certificate is almost always filled in long before the notarization. In fact, many preprinted certificates already have the venue locations typed in the blanks. Much of the time, this isn't a problem, because the agency drafting the document knows (more or less) where the notarization will be performed.

In the case of "less," you may need to correct the venue. If the state and county do not match where you are actually performing the notarization, line through the incorrect information, write in the correct state and county, and initial and date the correction. ■

100 Venue Split From Certificate

In many affidavits, the venue for the notarization may appear at the beginning of the document, separated from the jurat wording at the end of the affidavit by the affiants' statement. This is no cause for "separation anxiety." Such a "sandwich" format is very common with affidavits. ■

101 Notarizing Outside Of Your County

Every notarial certificate must have a venue ("State of _____, County of _____"), indicating where the notarization was performed.

YOU ARE HERE!

If you have statewide jurisdiction, the county you write in the venue will not necessarily be the same county that may be imprinted by your Notary seal or stamp, which is the county where your oath of office and/or bond have been filed. ■

ABOUT THE
NATIONAL NOTARY ASSOCIATION

The National Notary Association is the professional organization serving the nation's nearly five million Notaries Public with a wide variety of instructional programs and services.

As the nation's clearinghouse for information on notarial laws, customs and practices, the NNA educates its members through regular and special publications, seminars, an annual national conference and a host of educational services.

The Association is perhaps most widely known as the preeminent publisher of literature for and about Notaries. Major NNA publications include:

- *The National Notary* magazine
- *Notary Public Practices & Glossary*
- *State Notary Law Primers*
- *Notary Law & Practice: Cases & Materials*
- *Notary Home Study Course*
- *U.S. Notary Reference Manual*
- *Sorry, No Can Do!* Series

In addition, the NNA provides Notaries with the highest quality professional tools and supplies, including a popular instructional video series, seals, embossers, recordkeeping journals, fingerprinting devices and notarial certificates.

Though dedicated primarily to educating and assisting Notaries, the NNA devotes part of its resources to helping lawmakers draft notarial statutes and to informing the public about the Notary's vital role in modern society.

NATIONAL NOTARY ASSOCIATION
9350 De Soto Ave.
Chatsworth, CA 91311-4926
Telephone: (818) 739-4000
Fax: (800) 831-1211
Website: www.NationalNotary.org